MR. WORTHINGTON'S
BEAUTIFUL EXPERIMENTS
ON SPLASHES

GENINE LENTINE

MR. WORTHINGTON'S
BEAUTIFUL EXPERIMENTS
ON SPLASHES

GENINE LENTINE

NEW MICHIGAN PRESS
TUCSON, ARIZONA

NEW MICHIGAN PRESS

DEPT OF ENGLISH, P. O. BOX 210067

UNIVERSITY OF ARIZONA

TUCSON, AZ 85721-0067

<http://newmichiganpress.com/nmp>

Orders and queries to nmp@thediagram.com.

ISBN 978-1-934832-22-6. FIRST PRINTING.

Printed in the United States of America.

Design by Ander Monson.

Cover images courtesy of Amy Pryor, Detail from Skyblue, site-specific wall collage, 1999; and Hanneline Røgeberg, detail from Balzac IV, oil on canvas, 2007.

CONTENTS

I pass death with the dying, and birth with the new-washed babe,
    and am not contained between my hat and boots,
        —Walt Whitman, "Song of Myself"

These miracles we did; but now alas,
All measure, and all language, I should pass,
Should I tell what a miracle she was.
        —John Donne, "The Relic"

All things change into fire,
and fire exhausted,
falls back into things.
        —Heraclitus, "Fragment #22"

LOOTED

You are once again   rifling
  the sixth floor   supply cabinet.
Bethesda Naval   Hospital
Gyn/Onc ward.   Late, too late, to watch
  the babies sleep   three floors down.
Your mother breathes   with assistance
    in a single room   across the hall,
warm apparatus she needed   to give rise to you
  long since scooped   from her abdomen
  along with other   suspect tissue
      here   and there,
  her body's job   focused now
  on moving fluid   through her heart;
  blood to her brain   lets her raise her eyebrows
    when you lean   across the rail
and smooth her fore   head.
    Let her sleep,   your brother tells you
    as he dials   the room phone.
  Things seem   pretty stable here, he tells his wife,
See you soon.   What you have
    is this   supply closet:
pink square plastic   saline vials
for flushing the port   at her neck,
    good too   to carry in your backpack,
  for contacts;   syringes
for making a fine bead   of jade glue),
  silk suture thread (for sewing signatures).
You can do nothing to slow   the thicken-
  ing of blood in her   urine

2

as her systems re   cede, how it pools
like warm wax in the bed   side gauge,
but this packet of gauze, you can un   fold it
and stretch it thin   over bookboard.
You've adopted a striped hospital   robe as yours.
No one seems to care.   The nurses cluster
at their station and the war   d is quiet. You listen
for them, but they're used   to your being here
and you know where the apple   juice is
so you're no trouble. You   pocket
some surgical tape   for gift wrap.
Not an equal   trade for your mother,
but it's something.   You think you know
the inventory by now, but here's a new   low drawer
to investigate before padding   in these
disposable foam   slippers back
to the cot in her   room to sleep.
What   are these cool white
waffle weave cloths   , each folded
into its own cell   ophane bag?
(good for drawing?   ) But wait,
why is this one   closed at both ends?
Why this long   zipper?
Why this zipper   the length
of y   our mother's body?

INTERVIEW WITH THE PEAR TREE

When did you start making pears?

What is a pear?

(She runs her fingers over one
hanging on the branch.)

*Mmm. Yes. It began
before I could be seen,
when the great body rang,
striking, for the first time, the earth.
Over the long day, it lay in the sun,
and the birds came, and the flesh
fell away until all that was left
was the seed. Maybe it was
when the moon swelled
the seed, maybe
when the first true
leaf quickened.*

Did you always know you would make pears?

I wouldn't know how not to.

What is your process?

*I let the leaves
come to the branch
and when the bee is at the
blossom, I listen.*

Is dormancy difficult?

Dormancy?

A period when nothing happens.

(The tree pauses.)
I've never had one.

What about drought?

I spread my root hairs and wait.

Do you ever doubt?

When the bud breaks the green wood.

Do you ever think of making apples?

What is an apple?

Could you describe the kind of pears you make?

(A ripe pear drops into her upturned hands.)

PARTIAL INDEX, BY TITLE

Poem—

poem acting as a fire line
poem being held by the conductor
poem best enjoyed by date shown
poem bucking an evacuation order
poem carefully arranged to suggest a coastline
poem cast in an abandoned foundry
poem composed exclusively in civil twilight
poem composed of in excess of 60% post-consumer content
poem donated for this event by the House of Versace
poem drawn on an out-of-state bank
poem dripping from your _____
poem failing to notice its usual wish granted
poem founded on spectral evidence
poem hammered on adverse inference
poem held for questioning
poem in a handy refillable container
poem in place of pampas grass
poem jumping the fire line
poem knifing a seam in its paint-sealed window
poem laid in with a palette knife
poem made from what I had in the refrigerator
poem not realizing it's God
poem not realizing its god
poem not written chopping kubocha squash in 1/2-inch cubes
poem ruled inadmissible as hearsay
poem sheathed in heat-reflective wrap
poem slapped and salt-rubbed
poem stacked 25-deep on the runway

poem still awake after nightwatch
poem syllabically mimicking the poncho I crocheted in 7th grade
poem that can name three items in your purse
poem that didn't mean to hurt you
poem that does not have a ticket prior to boarding
poem that found its way in under the heatwrap
poem that guesses your weight (within 12 ounces)
poem that still only has a land line
poem that will be your substitute for today
poem that will pay you cash for your junk car
poem that would tell you if you had parsley in your teeth
poem that's still in the bathroom putting product in its hair
poem Vince thinks has had work done
poem visible only to the eyes of faith
poem whose ticket is not displayed at all times
poem with a living roof
poem with a preexisting condition
poem with a So-Cal style never prepared for the weather
poem with a suspicious thickening
poem with cradle-to-cradle certification
poem with dolphin-head terminals
poem with small parts that are a choking hazard
poem written into the bailout
poem, express—running on the local track

SOFTSOAP

The people of Softsoap stand ready at the faucet; they have seen how we suffer
and they want to help us　　　surmount the tender solitude
of washing our hands.　　　At such liminal moments our mind
becomes more spacious　　　and recalls the possibility of death.
Before this can get too traumatic, Softsoap holds out a small panda,
a transitional object　　　to broker the difficult realization.
The pump mechanism lifts　　　and drops the animal
through the clear liquid　　　as you press and release it.
Katherine says, No, what Softsoap is clearly doing at this vulnerable
juncture is seizing on　　　brand loyalty. To be spared
from the jaws of death　　　by a liquid soap, she ventures,
must imprint a deep　　　consumer bond. But what if
it's just that Softsoap worries the whole notion of liquid
is too scary for us—all that　　　indeterminacy, especially
after the small death　　　of peeing, is too much—and thus,
the need for this formal inter-　　　vention? Maybe it's a rickety bridge
phenomenon: how subjects, after crossing a bridge of fraying rope
rated the 8x10 glossies　　　they were shown as more attractive
than those very faces seen　　　again upon crossing a stone bridge.
You're in a meeting.　　　You excuse yourself.
The bathroom is quiet. This may be the only time in your day you are alone.
Your mind flickers,　　　and for a moment, rests
on the thought　　　you've been deferring since breakfast:
All this will be lost.　　　You stand up,
or if you're already standing, you step to the sink, somewhat changed,
and like Titania　　　what you see first is the animal.
It is beautiful to you.　　　*You will not die alone*, it promises.
I'm here; I'll see you through.　　　*Come on, let your thighs rest*

against the sink. Open your hands under this warm water. Yes, that's it. Briskly now—
rub them together—45 seconds   is recommended for proper antisepsis.
Good. Press your wet palms   together, fingertips up,
yes, hold them there   just in front of your face
and bend forward slightly   toward your reflection. Perfect.
Now, go on back out there and make that Powerpoint presentation, while you still can.

REGISTRY

You: you hold out your hand to receive it
but it spills over, your hand already full with it.

You: face to face with it,
you tell it you're looking for it.

You: you won't feel it as it's happening, but friends study
your face for what's different, ask if you got a haircut.

You: you'll forget it immediately,
but the interval before it happening again shortens.

You: you'll convince yourself it's happening when it's not.

You: you'll say it's not happening when it is.

You: you'll only recognize it happening to someone else.

Yours was stolen, you claim, and everyone you meet,
first thing you do is frisk them for it.

You: you had it once, you are prone to report,
and over and over you return to the dwindling site
to feel again the phantom limb pain.

You: when you're "outside," it's "inside."

You: when you're "inside," it's "inside."

You: you refuse to name it, but everyone turns
their heads together to you when someone asks who has it.

You: you say, *I won't talk about it.* But when you do talk about it—
which is all the time—you call it by a different name.

You don't deserve to have it, your story goes,
but when you're around, others say they have it.

You: you'll go on backburning after the fire's come through.

THE GOOD ARM

Huike cut off his own left arm. You know, that guy,
the second Zen ancestor, who stood in the snow
all night outside the door, and then at dawn,
drift at his waist, he cuts off his arm,
his blood pitting the snow? Always
the story tilts us toward the sev-
ered arm. We go right to the
sudden surge, to one drop
—— tunneling frozen
white ground; how
heat sinks into
cold. We've
been both:
snow and
blood so
we can
supply
memory.
I actually
dreamed it
one morning
just before waking,
upon waking, cradling,
my intact hand, in Brooklyn,
not in China, yes, testing fingers;
yes, it all still worked. In the dream,
my problem was: what to do with the hand?
Wrap it in white paper, store it in the produce
drawer while I find a more fitting disposition?

What *do* you do with the delusions you've
seen through? Deliver them to a designa-
ated site, like a varnish can on hazard-
ous waste pickup night? Or line
a pearwood box with cotton
batting, lay each one there
in turn, looking in on
them as needed, as
reminders? Cut-
ting off, at the
wrist, my
left hand,
swift irrevo-
cable gesture,
waking up, strok-
ing it, spared. We
hear the story: see how
he presents the arm? We try
on our own bodies, slip a foot
inside the foot of that one dispens-
able body standing all night at the door,
handing over a piece of itself, wiggle our toes
in that fresh body. *Am I ready to yield this,
just like that?* First, that's what I asked.
But now I'm more interested in the
other arm, the one, always off-
screen, that, in one stroke,
steered a carbon edge
  through its own

flesh, snapping
taut tendon
strings,
clean
through
radius, ulna.
Sipping marrow
up through the legs
the arm comes down
on itself. If it takes an arm
to sever an arm, what does that
leave? With what, other than the mind,
can the mind serve the mind? Riddled mind:
what we have, at hand, to unsnare riddled mind.

AS IT WILL

for Stanley Kunitz

Sometimes between one of Stanley's *Well's*
and whatever he says next,

there's ample space to take a nap—
it's late afternoon, and the porch is warm

and quiet—I can drift knowing
the front contour of his next word

will retrieve me when I'm needed,

and he will not have lost the thread
of my question. I don't fret neglecting

my work when this happens—I suspect half-
unconscious I can better communicate

with my employer. He's been contemplating
a passage marked "Continuity Beyond

the Body" for twenty minutes in silence

when he surfaces: *We know the conditions
for survival will pass,* he begins. *Eventually*

this planet earth will become uninhabitable.
When the sun grows cold, as it will,

the conditions for life will be irrevocable.
What are we going to do? he asks me.

Maybe I've been thinking too small,

calling around this morning trying
to find him a ride back to New York

in September. More mischief
sparking his voice this time, *What*

are we going to do about this? he presses.
I say, *We'll have to find another life*

form to inhabit. I say *All we can do*

is live fully until the sun cools,
and I remind him a lot will have happened

in the meantime, and there are other suns,
other stars. *They're a long way off,* he scoffs,

scattergaze not fixed on any one thing.
And then through the screen, a sharp shift

of light—a wolf spider quivers its web,

and though I'm never certain
what he's hearing or seeing, I know

it is this glint that has called him back
five-and-a-half billion years when he says, *Look.*

,

Comma, tongue
flick, drawn into
the white between
two phrases. De-
liberate, delicate,
graphite whisper,
you mark my page,
you urge my legs
open. Swim of the
head, the mouth
come to rest, caesura,
tip of the tuning
fork, crura humming,
vocal folds' taut bands
unstrummed,
universe, pause.

Comma, hand
at my shoulder
always coaxing
me back from headlong,
if I could learn your repose,
drop a plumb line into now,
I could live forever, or rather,
not mind if I didn't.
Crossing Sixth Avenue,
I felt for the first time
my foot declining
from curb to street,

my footfall on blacktop
sounding the bedrock below,
and a cab hauled past, sun
veering off the window.

In the bulldozed field
I hurried over red
clay in clumps, upturned
trunks, roots wrenched and
dried. And Stranger,
with your pulse of gold,
as always, you walked
two beats behind.
I leaned into my haste,
feet faltering
the altered terrain.
and then your touch,
and your voice:
Slow down some.
I bristled, then released
my momentum back,
and for a moment settled
there, here
in the curve of your palm,
and in front of me
where I was
rushing:

        sheer drop
        of empty space

SEVEN POSES:
DRAWN FROM THE MODEL

❧

Now the model is on hot sand. The
crocheted blanket digs into his knees.
He's caught, for this moment, his weary
course across the desert. No water in
sight. Nothing worth turning back for.
He leans into it, face turned in against
the sharp wind that breaks across his
skull. All the weight collecting in his
hands. The blood of the whole body
held in his hands.

❧

The pose seeks to catch the model
somewhere between where she thought
she was supposed to be and where she
thinks she is supposed to be.

❧

Pinky ring. Signet. His hand drapes
over the edge of the chair. Totally
languid, except he's flexing his toes on
his left foot. Is that part of the pose or
a reaction to the pose? A leak in the

pose? The place where his thought has
eddied. A reminder for himself, for us,
that he's still there though he may have
disappeared into the five-minute seam
that has opened up in time. The ring
speaks of a history. As does the path
the comb made in his hair before the
mirror. The powder along the crescent
of his [ass]. The way it whitens the skin
there. Eclipse. I can see him getting
ready this morning, the back edge of
his palm sliding smooth talc along the
seam. Preparing the body. Chalk line.
Buffer. Dusting. Light snowfall.

❧

Ten-minute pose. Some things have
been decided for me: the placement
of his palm against the belly of his
hamstring; the forward movement of
his leg; cant of his head; torsion of
spine and ribcage; how much time I've
been given to study this arrangement.
Sometimes it takes your own hand to
move your leg forward. (The lead line
wrapped around Buttercup's back legs
coaxing her across the paddock. How
she hopped her hooves ahead with
the pressure of the lead.) Where is
the model trying to go that he needs

a leather lead line looped around his leg? Or trying not to go? Where is he trying to stay? I told Richard, *You were my guide through the underworld.* He said, *Where are we now?*

❧

Seated pose. Stability of squared shoulders, hips, knees and feet. Dreamed this diagram: a line drawing, as in a dictionary, of a woman seated on a straight-backed chair. A double dotted line, indicating a band, starts at her pubic mound (and the word *mound* is somehow stressed) and ends at her mouth. Alongside it, a dotted arrow points up with an animated instruction: one firm swift lap of the tongue straight up the dotted line. *All One Stroke*, it emphasizes. Under the drawing, this brass label: PROSE.

❧

Today's timekeeper is Hal. He keeps consulting the wall clock, and for each pose, the egg timer rings a good minute before he calls time. It rings, winds down, and then stops ticking.

Hal doesn't hear well, Violet explains. Okay. So, the person in charge of time can't hear the bell. He does sense unerringly when the timer stops ticking, about a minute after the bell rings. Now another reclining pose. On her stomach, ankles crossed. Now the bell again. He turns toward it—but only to get his chamois. Another minute passes, and *Time!* Ten-minute pose. The model's cell phone is ringing. Much discussion about whether to turn it off or not. The most grievous model gaffe is puncturing the timeless agreement of the pose. But now suddenly I feel more interested in the pose. Avalokiteshvara, in the God realm, holding out time as a remedy. The timer rings again. Not a budge from our timekeeper. We've all learned this system, dismantling the strong Pavlovian response to a bell. We wait for the timer to run itself down. The absence of the ticking is what we listen for. The bell means nothing.

The model is lying on her back with her legs slung over to the right and her head turned to the left. I can feel the release, opening of the chest, twist of the spine, stretch along the side. Haptic knowledge. How does the drawing record that knowledge? What are the traces of subjective experience? Yesterday, when we did handstands against the wall in yoga, I loved pitching forward onto my hands, the feel of my legs balancing above my hips, the inversion of weight, the new relationship of blood and gravity. All day I kept replaying that action in my mind. All that was left was actually to do the handstand right there on Fifth Avenue. Now my hand is on Louie's head. Dog of miraculous comebacks. In my hand, all the dogs' heads I've held. Sweet tilt of his face. Maybe Selina can tell the neighbors he would have fewer problems if he weren't so good at living. Now he's pushing the full weight of his will into me. Right under my hand, what keeps him alive. Petting Louie has become my drawing.

MOLT

There was one moment
I was certain he loved me
by *loved* I mean *could see*
:
my pants
on the bathroom floor
in a heap, legs up
socks still holding
the form of my feet
waistband open against the tile
slipped off in one piece
and he came in to pee
as I stood under the shower
and then he stood over my pants
and asked me
pulling back the curtain
How did you do that?

THE GREAT DRAGON

(after physicist John Wheeler)

Human
armspan
always just shy
of its mass, you'll never
grasp both ends
at once, even
as its mid-rib presses
into your heart.

Look closely though:
the fingers of one
hand (you are
convinced) curl
over its teeth,
and the skin of your
other, skimming
scales, registers
categorically: whiptail.

And the space between:
smoky probability.

DEPENDS

I decided I'd try them
now—not wait,
shortcut decades
of suspense,
stay right here
at my desk,
instead of crossing
the room to pee.
Nothing else
changed, really.
Out the window, the breeze
continued lifting
each edge
of leaf. At first,
warm, kind of lovely,
so close against my skin;
and for the duration,
a feeling long familiar:
wet, uncomfortable, alive.

BROTHERS, IN SUCCESSION

one from behind
one from below

one seldom combed his hair
one folded his underwear

one was prone to orations
one clever at spatial relations

one had a knack for acrobatics
one a keen mind for mathematics

one angled three degrees to the right
one liked to try on my tights

one said I talked like their mother
on one, I performed the other

one made a habit of afternoon naps
one fancied the snug fit of straps

one conjured intricate tales
one once on deck watching whales

one in the barn
one on the train

one would do anything if shown
one night one made me drop the phone

one whispered technical terms
one down among mosses and ferns

One inquired *Who hurt you more*
One taped threats on the front door

SAMSARA IS NIRVANA

he   then
sto   od
be   fore
my   arm
ch   air
&   de-
mons
tra   ted
h   is
do   uble
zip   per
in   both
dire   ctions

28 MPH

I

—This morning I read in the *Times*
the *Book Review* section—
    —the average speed of ejaculation

II

is 28 Miles Per Hour—
    —How fast must thoughts come then?
I hadn't even finished the sentence—

III

    —and already: every detail perfect, I'm testing
a working model—
    —all that velocity in such close quarters!

IV

Why did I think of you then?—
    —That you could have that much speed in you!
I wouldn't want to be in the path—

V

    —of a Volkswagen at that speed
and you'd get a ticket if a strict cop clocked you—
    —at that clip in a school zone

VI

why did reading that—
      —in an instant deliver
one more way to want you—quick coalescent liquid you?

READ "THE WORLD"

For [you], I cast [the world]

—eye level   agave
has its own wrapping / *is* its own wrapping
between the wrapping and itself, nothing but itself
groove the blades make \ embossing self with self

plums jostle clean in a glass bowl of water
leafblade or plum—yes, closer, like that

pale green crown, glass bowl
I don't care what form you take this time   press
here on my shadow
I like it when you touch me there

everywhere casting

Would you mind standing here, where the planet would be?
where reality would be   if I let it?

let me list the ways I'd like to [   ]
let me list
let me
let
and now I've disappeared.
(what I've been wanting all along)
saying it, I'm back
(all along what) I've (been wanting)

let me list   rustle
your chapparal
divebell your vents

where I was standing—reality to be there

where I am standing—reality to be here

come here, speculative and spinning
come here, you flooded, burning rock

UPON YOUR "[UN]CONSOLABLE SADNESS"

"No creature ever comes short of its own completeness"
  —Dogen

un-? or is it *in-?*
Let it be *un-*
because it is animal
living outside the tent, stalking

un- or *in-*
is it (you) or (I)?

un- because it is also just a cloud, and you know it

Which is the fear? the *un-*
or the sadness itself?

Sadness, that won't kill you

but the *un-,*
to skid into that *un-*
and believe it, call that
crawlspace "the world"
maybe that's the only fear worth entertaining:
convinced to venture no further contact

I want to split it apart
un-*un* it of itself
two letters,
mirrored inversions

You say that word
and unspring the consoler

Upon this *un-*
I lay this quick reflex
(foolish, habitual)

Upon this *un-*
I lay this wish
for your head in my lap
consoling in degrees

, at least,

with small amusements,
what I can muster
to make a case for the world—
some facts about mammals:
this one lets half its brain sleep at a time
this one makes two kinds of milk,
one for the just born
one for the still suckling, or

who even needs so many cells?

Listen to this description of a protist,
and then try to say *unconsolable:*

Some possess a thrashing tail

or fine rhythmically beating hairs,
while others contain packets of chlorophyll...
I could go on,

or let's add a few more cells
and we have the volvox:

...a hollow sphere, where the wall
 is made up of cells,
each with a rhythmically beating hair
appearing like a tail.
The movement of the hairs
is coordinated to move
the entire sphere in one direction.

Okay.

Doesn't even that single beating hair
kind of cheer you up?

Ruiyan asked Yantou,
What is the fundamental constant principle?
Yantou said, *Moving*

See?
See?

Or something planetary in scope:
kneel here on this test-site soil
and here and here
wildfire and nuclear war, whatever sludge

you can point your tired finger to:
move your finger away to find

:grass

Ask it: it's not so bad is it? Being alive?

[whispered]
Did you know…?
Have you seen…?

Or little word jokes
Milena: *How do you spell D?*
until your smile taps
with its prospecting hammer
the *un-*'s rockface

moraine rent with a small white flower

slip my hand under the *un-*,
find where the *un-* gives

How about some formal puzzles
as on the NSA diagnostic test:

The top row of boxes follows a sequence.
Which box comes next?

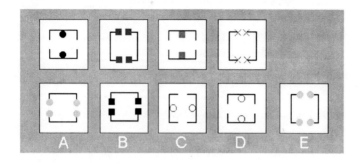

—consoling by giving your genius
something to do

Among the rarely bored
boredom can be mistaken for sadness

Yes, I know: *Picture this object*
rotated 45 degrees
what color is the side closest to you?

but the object is missing

It is, sometimes

but what about when it's there?

What happens

if you let it be there?

be subject?
Or, or,

We could try some
yogic breathing
that should do it

[V, at breakfast: *I just wanted to get you breathing again*]

Again, I see myself
wanting to make you see

You or I?

Until you pull the *un-* over your head
like an old sweater
or take the *un-* into you
as the nudibranch swallows poison
and turns it into color,

take your entire height
into the *un-*,
let the letters roll off you
until you can breathe again

Let the *un-*
stormsurge your slopes
let it uproot burned manzanita
let it all crash the guide walls

Who is being consoled?

And now?
Now what's happening?

And now, consolation sloshing
back onto the consoler

And now, hydrophobic soil
forkscored to receive some of it

There is nothing that can't be consoled
even if the last consolation registered is death
which asks nothing of us, only that we're here for it

Not this shed, burned to the ground
Not this melted lawn chair
its webbing one solid mass

in-? Let it be *un-*
I want some animal left in you
[like when you said, simply,
about my complaint of quaking:
Well, it's primal, the fear of death]

The person who,
when asked to name a fear,
holds out this:
Actually I don't have any—

lodging the sofa in front of the door—
I would never entrust
a burning building—my body—
to such a person

but when you said *un-*
unfurling each finger
as in Ramachandran's mirror box
opening to flat relief the "good hand"
my clenched phantom fist
could not help but open too
finally
when the good arm
is doubled and lets the brain see
what relief would look like

On a rainy morning, walking east
on Bleecker, I held out my arm
for a cab downtown to see Mark,
disappointed at everyone dying—
convinced of that—
but what about this rain, how it sheets
down that window, suggesting to the glass
a way to yield without shattering,
how a small surf crests on it (!)
And what am I to make of this cab driver
his sudden kindness, his swiftness
pulling over to me, *Come in out of that rain*

All that only made matters worse
because I couldn't make sense
of my "forsakenness,"
and the relentless kindness
how I felt one room over from it all
could hear it through the wall
but not be part of it

And I sat in Mark's office
and even before his—
how do you say?—
beautiful—face,
I could still say, *I feel inconsolable*

Inconsolable? You do?
Even to hear him repeat the word
consoled me. And I couldn't
offer you even this

When you said *un-*
I stood there silently

though everything in me felt called
toward this consolation
leaning into it
neither could I just receive it
without wanting to swoop onto it

as how whenever I see you I can't speak
and so I speak too much

or I want to strike the bell
with too much force
and so, barely touch it

UNSEEN PLANET

All I did was tilt my foot slightly
and the woman across the car stopped
           staring. Without even

looking up at her, I could feel her glance
lift, the mass and weight of it, like that ledge
           of current you can actually see

when a hawk scrambles up onto an air-
stream. I clear my throat and the man standing
           before me clears his, mirror

neurons sparking. Everyone's a stranger at first,
but by such a narrow margin. Stanley had a theory
           about the strangers in my dreams.

In one variation, the stranger sits at the edge
of the bed watching me sleep, but whatever
           the stranger does, it is with

a benevolence so thorough, it shocks me
awake. *Who was it do you think? Did you recognize
           the face?* he'd always ask.

The whole point is that they're strangers, I'd say,
but he had something very specific in mind.
           He'd never tell me what.

Next time check the face. Everyone's a stranger
at first. Who's next on the docket of strangers
          to be bumped up?

Most progress shown in: adjusting to a new situation.
Every time someone comes into this reading room
          I expect to know the person

and I look up and it's someone I've never seen. Are
there that many people in town? An exception is
          the woman I recognized the second

time she came in and went to the exact same (Dan
Brown) paperback on the spinning rack, picked it up
          and then put it back. I want

to sit here until I see someone I know or until the sun
goes down. *The only difference between drawing from life*
          and drawing from the imagination

is the time lapse is shorter. This is one of those quotes
with multiple attributions, like the one that's either
          Nelson Mandela or Marianne

Williamson. One putative source is a painter
whose work I'm not that into, so, having said that,
          I won't mention his name here;

it's more an indifference than an aversion, but given
that he allegedly said this, I leave more margin
          for one day seeing something I haven't

yet. Difference between a friend and a stranger: one
or two conversations. How many will it take to tip
          the spam filter? *Unseen planet*

creates a wobble. I want to sit here until I see someone
I already know or until the sun sets. At least
          on the way here, I saw Ricky.

We might not have even stopped to talk, but we
were both on our bikes riding toward each other
          and we kept veering in the same

direction to avoid crashing so finally we just stopped
in the middle of the street. He'd just been out
          in the harbor and saw three basking

sharks—a mother and two young ones. Don't worry
they only eat plankton, and he wasn't even swimming—
          though he could have been—

even in November, he dives in a "dry suit"—like a wet-
suit, but you can just zip it on right over your regular
          clothes. But this time

he was just out on the boat, so even if basking sharks
did have teeth instead of baleen, he'd have been in no
          danger. I know most of you

don't know him, but you could. What is not
going to happen in this poem is that it starts out
          remarking benignly on socioneuro-

logical microgestures and then suddenly someone you've
just met is getting sheared by a mother shark. You think
            you're all alone and the circulation

librarian says, *a book just came in for you* before you
hand her your card. *I spied a young cowboy all dressed
            in white linen.* You think you're alone

and the guy who asks for coins—(always *coins*
instead of *change*—*can you spare some coins?*) on Sixth
            & Tenth, one morning, tells you,

Girl, I thought you'd never come out of that post office!
My brother has never gotten over the sting
            of being spam-filtered. It leaves

a faint imprint, like those stories of people
standing next to a tree when lightning strikes, who
            unbutton their shirt and reveal

the outline of the tree on their breast. *Unseen
planet creates a wobble.* That teacup chihauhua
            next door named Kilo, usually

he won't let anyone pet him, but he *really* likes you!
To View the suspect message, click this link:
            Subject: Thinking of you…

FINDINGS FROM THE *SPIRIT* ROVER

What I saw last, I'll give you first: aluminum canister of holy water
on my grandmother's closet shelf. My father's written right on it: *Lourdes*
Years, it's been there, above the neat row of hangers holding killer

polyester slacksuits. When did he notice it once held insect-
icide? Did that, for a moment, deter him? In the holiday hangar, a flying
"Inflatable lady" floats beside a space capsule. Is this dented Raid

can all he could find? He rattled the patio door, dreamed of the nightraid.
I drag a strand of hair through the bathwater to see if I can stretch water.
My 2nd grade valentine: "I've looked all over for you," (diecut pilot flying

a cockeyed spaceship.) Flannery O'Connor wrote to her friend, *Lourdes*
was not as bad as I expected, I took the bath, for a selection of bad motives.
We took the canister to the patio to photograph it. I turned killer

to the camera, so what you see looking at it head on is *killer*,
and if we take the cap to be a clock, screenprinted at midnight: raid.
She tells me, *You can't just drink it, you have to show it some respect,*

raising a clear column, offering me a taste of concentrated water.
My hold has come in at the library: *Song of Bernadette of Lourdes*
on DVD. Of course, the ones who most believe her say she's lying.

Always a new relic in his flight bag when he came home from flying
missions. Must be my mother made me this natural born speller:
what he actually wrote was L - O - U - D - R - E - S.

Snickers and Mars bars, a chunk of a pyramid marked in pencil: *PYraMidS,
Egypt. Ashes from Mt. Vesuv. March 1944* in a glass Alka-Seltzer
jar, *days 23, 25, 26,* in his hand on the label. Days spent erupting. I inspect

the bottled landscape, sealed 60 years. Tiny lunar rovers modeled after insects—
falling engineered into their stride to manage the terrain, falling :: flying.
In one scene: Bernadette on her knees eating mud in her faith for water.

The North Vietnamese had a saying: *The man in the sky is a killer.*
Last night in Grace's book I found this, and in Bernadette's letters I read,
Everything is nothing to me—after seeing "the lady" at Lourdes—

Neither ideas nor emotions, neither honor nor sufferings. Even Lourdes water
now banned from carry-ons; I left the canister with my cousin.
Long gone, the one body marked *my father. Spirit* sent back samples
only of ash. *Opportunity,* evidence, from its tracings, of liquid water.

MY FATHER'S COMB

Black plastic
raised letters
proclaimed it
unbreakable
and so I began
to bend the un-
relenting spine.
First nothing,
then a little give,
heat at the seam,
blanching
at the faultline.
Half an hour
at his mirror, I
worked at it.
I worked it away
from me and
back. I worked
at the word
until the word,
until the atom
of its lie split,
until the word
broke in my hands.

FIFTEEN THOUSAND USEFUL PHRASES

(after Grenville Kleiser)

❧

It's sweet, really, how you arrange them
alphabetically, as if I could go to your book,
seeking precision and find something
there under, say, "M:"
Memory was busy at her heart.

You have this notion
that phrases, used correctly,
could actually do something useful.
It's right there on the cover, *useful*
uncomplicatedly predicated of *phrases.*

I want to believe you.
Browsing the chapters: *Significant Phrases,*
Impressive Phrases, Felicitous Phrases,
I feel your *absolute, complete, unqualified and final*
confidence that fifteen minutes a day
more effectively than an hour a day of desultory reading
will equip the reader, me
for a life of clear expression.

We just need to read the phrases:
    intimations of unpenetrated mysteries
    dark with unutterable sorrows
    days that are brief and shadowed

find where they fit,
and our conversation will sparkle.

Striking Similes
you imagine we might memorize,
the perfect clothes
for our ideas
    as silent as the sheeted dead
    all unconscious as a flower
    like dining with a ghost.

❦

I have to ask you,
What is your pose on perfect expression now?

Say any one of these phrases.
Say three in a row.
They fill the air for a moment
and then they are gone.
Like dining with a ghost,
but in reverse:
the food is disappearing;
you can see it happening,
and you are left, across the table.
Something has been transacted.
The plate is empty. Is someone there?
Did someone say something? Did anyone hear?

Maybe in *Conversational Phrases*,
I could find something to say to her, now
after a long unaccustomed silence:

> *but who could foresee what was going to happen?*

or

> *Will you have the kindness to explain?*

or

> *It's a difficult and delicate matter to discuss.*

or

> I hate that you fucked him in our bed.

I browse the book, every page a distraction;
what I find are my own formulations,
the consequences of an agitated mind.

Something made of language is gone
even as it's spoken.
I dreamed I was rinsing words from a sponge.

I'll show you some useful things:
a hammer, a tent, a compass,
even the paper this poem is printed on.
I swear to God
I was walking home at midnight
and had nothing but a draft of this poem
and I had to use it to clean up after my dog.
I felt the warmth spread through the paper's grain
and it wasn't just an *idea* of warmth.

I look to you.
I entreat you.

What could you say in answer?
Tell me, "*I have a secret: a whole chapter of blank pages.*"
Tell me, "*I had my moments when my faith flagged. Here, look where I
    throw it all away*
*and just say "some" instead of reaching for the loved particular: 'as quick
    as the movement*
*of some wild animal' or 'The earth was like a frying pan or some such
    hissing matter,'*
*as much as I despised the indefinite. Or when I just repeat myself:
    'slender and thin*
as a slender wire.' You get the idea, don't you?

*Read the phrases aloud. Listen to that space where one phrase ends and
    another begins.*
Big expanse of space. That's what I say now."

❧

And my mother said, *You won't find me*
in code. Don't look for me
in the words of your child.
She, who filled our house with talk, told me:
Listen. If you want to know I'm there,
just make yourself quiet.

A task for you: Try to describe for me
how this dog arranges her limbs on the couch,

how one paw has slipped between the cushions,
and something about how her ribs expand.
Let me see the slope of her skull. Oh, and
please include how the couch is almost exactly
her color, try to show me that color,
that of the couch, and the difference between the two.
See if you can delineate the fine articulations of her spine—
and try to do it without asking me to look at something else.

Tell me,
even your name fails you. Grenville?
I'm going to call you something else,
you don't mind do you?
Spirit of Capture, Hope, Faith.
What is there in your name,
its initial consonant clusters, its word-final liquids
that has anything to do with you?

And so, I'm sure you won't mind
if I just call you, say, Byron or Sebastian,
or why not even my own name, Genine?

❧

I want to ask you
Could you stand the shifting?

Just today on the street
I thought I heard hatred in the contour of a vowel,
a wife leaning into her husband, lowered voice,
Did you see him, there, that one with the purple towel?
I tried to track it, in the falling intonation,
the twisted arc of her sigh.
And I had just seen him too and what I mainly registered
was a luxury of skin, a graceful body walking alone
except for his dog, and he had tied a cloth
around his hips so it sloped to a knot,
which I have since slipped open over and over
just to watch it fall. And it was private;
I had no one to tell, so he remained for me
without language.

But I felt, even as I passed him,
the urge to assign some words.

And I can bring this before you now,
this detail: his puppy tumbling,
five steps for every one of his, the leash taut.
I had to admire the precision
of the draping, the assertion of his long stride
through the cloth's steep gap.

I could have just received it, but *gorgeous* and *sweep* and *oh* and
I think I actually drew in a breath.

And when I got further down the street
and saw them leaning in, I knew why.

And I wanted to tell the woman
It wasn't a *towel*. Have you ever seen a towel that size?
Or would a towel hang with such elegance?
And, could a towel come to so fine a knot?

But she denied you
your promise; she did not pursue
the right word,
as if the imprecision put her at a wanted distance from him,
and her husband listened and nodded as if he understood.
I wanted to tell her, *No, it wasn't a towel,*
but I didn't even want to name it.
Sometimes I wish for no language;
I want my whole job to be seeing.
But let's say the word is *sarong.*

Now we're in the marketplace;
we're off his thigh,
in a bright noisy store, packed with racks, all one price.
And if I do say *sarong,*
I'll say it mainly for the pleasure of feeling
my tongue arch along my palate. And I'll know
that what I saw is already in the past
the second I try to put a word on it anyway.
Just look.

But she didn't even give him that.
Maybe she didn't like the *idea* of him,
his valent body,
the confusion of signifiers.

Skirt with no shirt, and then the sigh.

And still they stopped walking
to lean into each other.
I took the permission of the street
to stand there next to them,
nothing to do but listen,
long enough to hear her skid
to the end of her sentiment
and her sigh said, *That's no son of mine.*

❦

I imagine you were happy
in your dream of precision.
I am touched by your faith in the alphabet.

And you're long gone
and I address you here, what's left of you,
in your binding.
There is some use in that, isn't there?
Just the idea of your book was enough
to make someone buy it new in 1918.
And then again, eighty years later, I could find it,
and I admit it was mainly an amusement,
but I *was* curious.

I want to believe you; can you show me again
the part about how ideas can be clothed?
And I'll show you how it's all drag,
the moment it passes from thought to form.

Look, you know I loved finding *meadow*
when my lips grazed the surface of her skin
where her jaw meets her throat

and I know I loved
how having a word for it right there
let me tell her this, let me whisper it right there
where my mouth was
and bring her into the sun-bending grass
in the darkness of our bed.

And I have heard you, you tell me, *speaking in a garden at a
    memorial for a friend, younger*
*than her mother was when she gave birth to her, whose numerous
    tumors crowded the cavities*
*of her body and wrapped her aorta, diminishing her before her own
    two daughters' eyes.*
And I have seen you visit her there on her couch and you thought,
    She's a leaf blown against
a sheet of glass, *and somehow thinking that made it more manageable.*

And yes, she told her mother, *I want Genine to do something.*
And I took that to mean, *I want Genine to say something.*
And yes, I made sure when I spoke
to the group gathered in the sloping shade
that I said *radiant* when I related my dream
of her dancing down her narrow street
because wouldn't her mother want for that moment—
as long as it took to say the word—
for the sun to be blasting all its light on her daughter
now that she couldn't wet her child's mouth
with water drawn through a thin straw?

And didn't you listen with me
when an M.I.T. syntactician
told the tale of a dying warrior chief
who possessed a word capable of killing,
and needed to pass it on before he died?
He gathered the children of the village
around his bed and gave them each a baby chick,
then told them
                    Now, crush it in your hand.
And all but one snapped the fine bones
easily. And that one received the word
because he could manage its power.

And I was soaked in that belief.
And I wanted to be that child.

And the coat check clerk told me,
Describe it and you can have it back.

So, it's not as if I don't see your point.

But in your stockpile of expression,
can I find a way to get the gist
of this white peach I'm eating?

And for example, most of what I say is lost
on my dog, and she seems *fine.*

❦

And what about there,
right at the end
of my mother's life,
when she finally
stopped talking,
when she stopped
loading her breaths
with language
and we exchanged breath
like conversation,
reversed
from my birth
when what I did was gasp
for air with no words available.

And you say,
*See, there? See the child trade breaths with her mother, and then when
  the one stops,
the other waits, and when nothing comes, watch how the child takes her
  first breath
again, alone.*

And haven't I taken a word on my tongue
and held it there waiting
for a breath to come carry it away?

You know I want to find a way to capture
the grace of his stride,
the exact quality of light on his skin.
I want to go back onto the street
and find the moment frozen there
so I can get it all down, *better* this time.

I want to see my own face in seeing

and disappear into the telling
so that you can see through me.
And even better if I'm glass
and if what you see is slightly more,
if there's a little refraction, more heat.

WILLAMETTE METEORITE

(Rose Center for Earth and Space, NYC)

All day   children
    they touch me without stopping
      their questions and chatter
They touch me and their questions stop
    Their hands all day inside these cavities
      and for a moment they are silent
annulus of a wave
    then their voices begin again
I am a shattered remnant
    of a planet, nickel iron core of a planet
    here I have length and height
        I have *weight: 15.5 tons*
    Here, I am a *specimen*
  I am *rare and important*
    I should say, *metallic iron meteorites are a relatively rare kind* here
      Imagine, traveling this far, and for so long
First the main shock of shattering,
    then two subsequent shocks
      one of which knocked me here
  I'm among the largest meteorites found
    Of what was never found I am not the largest
    not the smallest either
These cavities—don't think that's some kind of
    outer space thing   That's local rain, and oxygen
    That came from sitting in one place, exposed
    The first ones dipped their arrowheads
      in the water
      collecting in my crevices

They'd drink it   spoon it into their sick
    Of course it changes them
            makes them more like themselves
Once, I never stopped moving
    I didn't have these edges,   or anything that might provoke a name
    It was pure contiguity, then fire
                            One day a tiny dog
wriggled from a handbag   cold salt nose   and before anyone could see
        he peed on me   I liked it, actually
    Otherwise, no rain   no fire
            Why do you insist we are different?
    Here, put your cheek
            Put your hand here
                just above the solid part
        float it there
            without touching   Do you feel that hum
                    in the sponge
                        of your bones?

ACKNOWLEDGMENTS

These poems only faintly register the full fortune of friendship. To express thanks is to abandon any attempt at proportion, to reconcile myself to any notion that my thanks might be adequate to what I receive daily, let alone all I am offered—inspiration, sustenance, pushback—and am not able to take in. From within this overflow, Thank you to Ernest + Lynn Ackermann, Rev. Victoria Austin, Lisa Andrews, Susan Brennan, Lee Briccetti, Bobbie Bristol, Olga Broumas, Sommer Browning, Mark Doty, Sherry Dowdy, Erica Ehrenberg, Liz Eitt, Thomas Sayers Ellis, Mark Epstein, Nick Flynn, Debra Gitterman, Louise Glück, Eamon Grennan, Amy Gross, Rev. Paul Haller, Rev. Blanche Hartman, Headlands staff, Jane Hirshfield, Amy Hosig, Marie Howe, Major Jackson, Tyehimba Jess, Elizabeth King, Galway Kinnell, Alix Lambert, Phillis Levin, Jennie Livingston, Daria Martin, Richard McCann, W. S. Merwin, Martin Moran, Naomi Shihab Nye, Roshi Enkyo O'Hara, Sensei Joshin O'Hara, Sharon Olds, Judith Parker, Amy Pryor, Frances Richard, Marnie Crawford Samuelson, Shradha Shah, Laurie Sheck, Renée Soto, Brother David Steindl-Rast, Robert Thurman, Mary-Elizabeth Tiller, Tofu-A-Go-Go, Alice Quinn, SFZC + VZ friends, Alan Shapiro, Jean Valentine, Margo Viscusi, Claire Willis, Donna Wyant, C.D. Wright, and others too numerous to include here.

Ongoing gratitude to Marion and Joseph Lentine + fellow offspring thereof, for grace; Ander Monson, for exquisite attention to [ ]; and for all your contributions to the cover, thank you to Ellen Fullman and Theresa Wong, for composure; Hanneline Røgeberg, for volume and possibility; Amy Pryor, for this sky;

and to Stanley Kunitz, curious being, for being curious, always.

NOTES

These poems have appeared in the following journals, sometimes in different versions: "Molt," *Gulf Coast;* "Interview with the Pear Tree," "My Father's Comb" *DIAGRAM;* "Seven Poses: Drawn from the Model," *Ninth Letter.*

The logic problem on page 38 is reproduced with permission from the University of Kent Careers Advisory Service. (www.kent. ac.uk/careers Contact bw@kent.ac.uk).

The title of this book comes from the book *On Growth and Form* by D'Arcy Wentworth Thompson. (New York: Dover, 1992. Originally published by Cambridge University Press, 1942)

"28 MPH": Thanks to Thomas Sayers Ellis for slowing this poem down.

In "Upon Your '[Un]consolable Sadness,'" I used selections from the following sources: Dogen Zenji, *Shobogenzo,* Genjokoan; *Book of Serenity,* tr. Thomas Cleary; Case #75, "Ruiyan's Constant Principle," Lindisfarne Press, 1990: 316; Andrew Parker, *In the Blink of an Eye,* New York: Basis Books, 2004: 15-16; and V.S. Ramachandran, *A Brief Tour of Human Consciousness,* New York: Pi Press: 15.

GENINE LENTINE's poems, essays, and interviews have appeared in *American Poetry Review, American Speech, DIAGRAM, Gulf Coast, Ninth Letter, O, the Oprah Magazine,* and *Tricycle. The Wild Braid: A Poet Reflects on a Century in the Garden,* her collaboration with Stanley Kunitz and photographer Marnie Crawford Samuelson was published by W.W. Norton in 2005. Ongoing projects include *Listening Booth, Spacewalks,* and *The Heinous Task Table,* all of which took shape in a 2009 Project Space residency at the Headlands Center for the Arts. She has an MFA in Poetry from NYU, as well as an M.S. in Theoretical Linguistics from Georgetown University. She is the Artist-in-Residence at the San Francisco Zen Center for 2009-10.

NEW MICHIGAN PRESS, based in Tucson, Arizona, prints poetry and prose chapbooks, especially work that transcends traditional genre. Together with DIAGRAM, NMP sponsors a yearly chapbook competition. Genine was a finalist in 2009.

DIAGRAM, a journal of text, art, and schematic, is published bimonthly at THEDIAGRAM.COM. Periodic print anthologies are available from the New Michigan Press.

COLOPHON

Text is set in a digital version of Jenson, designed by Robert Slimbach in 1996, and based on the work of punchcutter, printer, and publisher Nicolas Jenson.

Breinigsville, PA USA
27 January 2010
231443BV00001B/74/P